WiderWorld

POWERED BY

Practice Tests Plus

EXAM PRACTICE

CAMBRIDGE ENGLISH KEY FOR SCHOOLS

Pearson Education Limited
Edinburgh Gate
Harlow
Essex CM20 2JE
and Associated Companies throughout the world.

First published 2016

ISBN: 978-1-292-10726-4
(Parts of Test 1 and Test 2 taken from Practice Tests Plus Cambridge English Key for Schools with Key)

Set in Arial
Printed in Great Britain by Ashford Colour Press Ltd

Photo acknowledgements
The publisher would like to thank the following for their kind permission to reproduce their photographs:

(Key: b-bottom; c-centre; l-left; r-right; t-top)

Corbis: 32r; **Fotolia.com:** ArtmannWitte 29, redleg 34, Tiler84 32tl; **Pearson Education Ltd:** 46, Tudor Photography 9; **Rex Shutterstock:** Ian Bird 12, Sipa Press 14

All other images © Pearson Education

Contents

Exam Overview

The **Cambridge English: Key for Schools** exam, also known as the **Key English Test (KET) for Schools** is an examination set at **A2 level** of the Common European Framework of Reference for Languages (CEFR). It is made up of **three papers**, each testing a different area of ability in English: Reading and Writing, Listening, and Speaking. Reading and Writing carry 50% of the marks; Listening and Speaking carry 25% of the marks each.

Reading and Writing   1 hour 10 minutes

Listening   30 minutes (approximately)

Speaking   8–10 minutes (for each pair of students)

All the examination questions are task-based. Rubrics (instructions) are important and should be read carefully. They set the context and give important information about the tasks. There is a separate answer sheet for recording answers for the Reading and Writing paper.

Paper	Format	Task focus
Reading and Writing Nine tasks 56 questions	**Part 1: matching.** Matching five sentences to eight notices, plus one example.	**Part 1:** reading short texts for the main message.
	Part 2: three-option multiple choice sentences. Reading five sentences on a related topic and selecting the correct answer.	**Part 2**: reading and identifying appropriate vocabulary
	Part 3: three-option multiple choice and matching. Five multiple-choice items. Five matching items in a dialogue, selecting from eight possible responses.	**Part 3:** functional language. Identifying an appropriate response.
	Part 4: right/wrong/doesn't say or **three-option multiple choice.** Seven items on one long text or three short texts.	**Part 4:** reading for detailed understanding and main idea.
	Part 5: three-option multiple choice cloze. Reading a text with eight gaps and selecting the correct word to complete each gap.	**Part 5:** reading and identifying appropriate structural words.
	Part 6: word completion. Five words to complete, using a definition.	**Part 6:** identifying appropriate item and spelling.
	Part 7: open cloze. Short text with ten gaps. Completing the text with one word in each gap.	**Part 7:** reading and identifying appropriate words.
	Part 8: information transfer. Two short texts to prompt completion of a third text with five gaps. Completing the text with words or numbers.	**Part 8:** reading with focus on content and accuracy.
	Part 9: guided writing. Short text or rubric to prompt written response. Three messages to communicate.	**Part 9:** Writing a short note, email or postcard of 25–35 words.

Paper	Format	Task focus
Listening Five tasks 25 questions	**Part 1: three-option multiple choice.** Listening to five short dialogues and choosing the correct picture for each answer.	**Part 1:** listening to identify key information.
	Part 2: matching. Listening to a longer dialogue and matching five items with eight options.	**Part 2:** listening to identify key information.
	Part 3: three-option multiple choice. Listening to a longer dialogue and choosing the correct answer for five items.	**Part 3:** listening to identify key information.
	Part 4: gap-fill. Listening to a longer dialogue and writing the missing word(s) or number in five gaps.	**Part 4:** listening and writing down information.
	Part 5: gap-fill. Listening to a longer dialogue and writing the missing word(s) or number in five gaps.	**Part 5:** listening and writing down information.
Speaking Two tasks	**Part 1: examiner-led conversation.**	**Part 1:** giving personal information.
	Part 2: two-way conversation with visual and written prompt.	**Part 2:** giving factual information related to daily life.

Practice Test 1 with Guidance

Parts 1–9

About the paper

The *Reading and Writing* paper lasts for one hour and ten minutes. It contains nine parts and has a total of 56 questions. There are a range of text types and a variety of question types.

Part 1: Signs

In Part 1, you read eight short texts (usually signs and notices found in schools, railway stations, airports, shops and on roads, for example) and five sentences that explain the signs and notices. You have to match the five sentences to the eight short texts. This part tests your ability to understand the main message of a very short text.

Part 2: Topic vocabulary

In Part 2, you read five sentences with gaps. The sentences are linked by topic or story line. You have to fill the gap by choosing the best word (A, B or C). These words are verbs, nouns or adjectives. This part tests your ability to read and choose appropriate vocabulary.

Part 3: Everyday conversations

Part 3 has two tasks. For questions 11–15, you choose the best option (A, B or C) to complete five two-line conversations. For questions 16–20 you choose from a list of eight options to complete a longer conversation. There are three extra options that you do not use. This part tests your ability to understand language used in everyday conversations.

Part 4: Factual text

In Part 4, you read one long text or three short newspaper or magazine articles and answer seven questions. There are two possible formats to the questions: a) decide whether the statements are right, wrong or the text doesn't say; b) choose the right option from A, B or C. Part 4 tests your ability to understand main ideas and some details of a longer text.

Part 5: Factual text

In Part 5, you read one long text, e.g. a newspaper/magazine article or encyclopaedia entry. The text has eight gaps and you need to choose the right word (A, B or C) to complete the text. This part tests your use of grammar (e.g. verb forms, auxiliary verbs, determiners, pronouns, prepositions and connectives).

Part 6: Word completion

In Part 6, you read five definitions and complete five words which are related by topic (e.g. food, education). You have to spell the word correctly. There is one space for each letter of the word and the first letter of the word is given to you. Part 6 tests your ability to read and identify the right word and your ability to spell that word correctly.

Part 7: Notes, short message, letter

In Part 7, you read a short text, usually a note, letter or email, with ten gaps. You have to think of one word to fit each gap. This part tests your use of grammar and vocabulary, as well as your spelling (you must spell the missing word correctly).

Part 8: Information transfer

In Part 8, you read two short texts (e.g. emails, adverts) and you use the information to complete a short text (e.g. a form, a note, a diary). You have to complete five spaces with one or more words or numbers, spelled correctly. Part 8 tests your ability to read and understand short texts, and to write down words, phrases or numbers (not sentences) to complete a different type of text.

Part 9: Continuous writing

In Part 9, you write a short message (an email, note or postcard) of 25–35 words. You are given a short text (a note, an email or a postcard) or some instructions which tell you what you need to write. This part tests your ability to communicate a short written message to a friend.

Part 1

- Read the instructions and example carefully first.
- Read the sentences and short texts carefully. Think about where you might find such texts.
- The signs and notices may contain words which you do not know, but this should not stop you from understanding the main message.
- You may see the same word appear in a sign/notice and in a sentence. You need to be careful. This does not mean it is the answer. It is important that you understand the meaning of the sentence in order to be able to match it to a sign/notice.

Part 2

- Read the instructions and the example sentence before you begin. That way you will know the story line or the topic of the sentences.
- For each question, read the whole sentence first to get a general understanding.
- Read the sentence again and try to predict what the missing word might be.
- Look at the options (A–D) and decide which one fits the gap.
- Read the sentence again to make sure it makes sense.
- If you are not sure which word to choose, decide which options are clearly wrong, and then see which are left. If you're still not sure, you should guess. You do not lose marks for wrong answers, and your guess may be right.

Part 3

- Read the instructions and the example for questions 11–15.
- Read each of the questions/statements carefully. Think about who might be asking the question or saying the statement and how you might respond to it.
- Read each option (A–C) carefully and decide which is the best response. When you have decided on an option, read the conversation carefully to make sure it makes sense.
- For questions 16–20, read the instructions and the example to understand who is talking and where they are.
- Read the gapped conversation on the left-hand side first to get an idea of what is said in the conversation.
- Read what the first speaker says before and after each gap carefully before choosing the best response (A–H) for the gap.
- When you have completed the dialogue, read it all carefully to make sure it makes sense.

Part 4

- Read the instructions carefully. They tell you what the text is about.
- Read the text quickly to get the general meaning. The text will contain words you don't know. Don't worry about these. You can still answer the questions.
- Read the example and try to see where the answer is located in the text.
- Read the questions carefully and underline the key words. These should help you scan the text to locate the information you need to answer the questions.
- The questions follow the order of the information in the text, so answer them in order.
- Read the text again to find answers to the questions.
- Answer option 'Wrong' means the information in the text is different to the information in the question. Answer option 'Doesn't say' means that the question asks for information that is not in the text.

Part 5

- Read the instructions carefully to get an idea of the topic.
- Then read the whole text quickly, ignoring the gaps, to get a general understanding.
- Read the text again. At each space, stop and try to predict what the missing word might be.
- Look at the options (A–C) and decide which one fits the gap. Look at the whole sentence to check the meaning of the missing word.
- If you are not sure which word to choose, decide which options are clearly wrong, and then see which are left. If you're still not sure, you should guess. You do not lose marks for wrong answers, and your guess may be right.
- When you have finished, read the whole text again and check that it makes sense.

Part 6

- Read the instructions carefully. They give you the topic that the words all relate to.
- Read each definition carefully. Try to work out if the word is a noun, verb or adjective.
- Remember, the topic is given to you. It might help you to think of the word in your own language first.
- Make sure you spell the missing word correctly. Mistakes in spelling are penalised.

Part 7

- Read the whole text first to get the general meaning.
- Read the whole sentence containing the gap before deciding on the right word. Think about the type of word it is.
- Make sure you spell the missing word correctly. Mistakes in spelling are penalised.
- When you've finished, read the whole text again to make sure it makes sense.

Part 8

- Read the instructions and input texts. Then, look at the example and the writing task carefully.
- You need to understand the vocabulary required to fill in forms or to take notes. For example, name, surname, date of birth, age, address, date, time, cost.
- The texts may contain two names, two dates, two prices, etc. Read the texts carefully to decide which one is correct.
- Write the correct information in the space.
- Correct spelling is important, so make sure you copy the words correctly.

Part 9

- Read the instructions and/or input text carefully. They tell you what type of message you need to write, who it is for and what kind of information you should include.
- There will always be three things that you need to communicate in your answer.
- If there are only instructions, you must address the prompts in the instructions **in order**.
- If there is a short input text, you must respond appropriately to all three elements it contains.
- You need to write between 25 and 35 words, so count them carefully. Remember to start with a greeting (e.g. *Hi Anna*) and to add your name to sign off at the end.

Part 1

Tip strip

Question 1
How do you show the teacher you want to answer in class?

Question 2
Why not? What's the opposite of *noisy*?

Question 3
Look for words for clothes in the notices.

Question 4
What's the opposite of *found*? Look for a phone number.

Question 5
Which notice has the name of a sport and a time?

Questions 1–5

Which notice (**A–H**) says this (**1–5**)?
For questions **1–5**, mark the correct letter **A–H** on your answer sheet.

Example:

0   You must not eat
or drink in here.

---

1   You should not call out
an answer.

A   NO FOOD OR DRINKS IN THE
CLASSROOM

2   You must not make any
noise.

B   Want to say something?
Raise your hand

3   You must not bring these
items of clothing into the
classroom.

C   *Walk don't run*

D   Tennis lessons for kids
Every Saturday morning at 9.00

4   Call this number if you
have found something.

E   Hang coats and jackets
in the hall

5   Be here at this time if you
want to learn how to play
this sport.

F   Test in progress
Please be quiet

G   *LOST*
A black and white pencil case
Call Fiona 0789654334

H   Found something that's not yours?
Tell your teacher.

Part 2

Questions 6–10

Read the sentences about a boy called Daniel.
Choose the best word (**A**, **B** or **C**) for each space.
For questions **6–10**, mark **A**, **B** or **C** on your answer sheet.

Example:

0 Daniel and his family have just moved to a new ....

   A town   **B** neighbour   **C** countryside

0	A	B	C
	▬	▭	▭

---

6 Like many kids his age, Daniel enjoys .... video games.

   A doing   **B** making   **C** playing

7 He has made a new .... at school, Paul.

   A boy   **B** student   **C** friend

8 In the morning, Daniel and Paul .... to school on foot.

   A take   **B** come   **C** go

9 They also play football together at the ....

   A weekend   **B** day   **C** afternoon

10 They like spending their .... time together.

   A free   **B** busy   **C** day

Tip strip

For all of these questions, think about verb patterns. Try saying the complete sentences silently to yourself. Do they sound correct?

Question 6
Which verb goes with *game* or a sport like *tennis*?

Question 7
What happens when you meet new people that you like?

Question 8
Which verb means *travel*?

Question 9
The expression *at the* only goes with one of the options. Also, think about when people have more time.

Question 10
What's the word for the time when we are not working or studying?

Tip strip

Question 11
The answer includes the name of a person.

Question 12
The answer means 'I agree'.

Question 15
Look for an answer that gives a reason.

Questions 11–15

Complete the five conversations.
For questions **11–15**, mark **A**, **B** or **C** on your answer sheet.

Example:

0

---

11 Whose bag is that?

    A Sally's, I think.

    B Yes, it is.

    C It's not me.

12 Let's call Samantha to see what she's doing.

    A Not bad.

    B I hope so.

    C Good idea.

13 How are you feeling?

    A Much better, thank you.

    B I don't think so.

    C I don't feel like it.

14 I have to go and do my homework now.

    A Have you finished?

    B Do you like it?

    C I'll see you later.

15 Why didn't you come to my party?

    A I didn't like it.

    B I wasn't feeling well.

    C I had a great time.

Part 3

Questions 16–20

Complete the phone conversation between two friends.
What does Yolanda say to Maria?
For questions **16–20**, mark the correct letter **A–H** on your answer sheet.

Example:

Maria: Hi, Yolanda. It's Maria.

Yolanda: **0** .....*D*.....

Maria: Really? I was calling to see what you were doing on Saturday.

Yolanda: **16** ....

Maria: Oh, I need to get some too. I was thinking about seeing a film.

Yolanda: **17** ....

Maria: I can't. I'll be playing in the basketball final.

Yolanda: **18** ....

Maria: Yes, and I was hoping you could come.

Yolanda: **19** ....

Maria: Great! I'll see you on Sunday then.

Yolanda: **20** ....

A My mum and I are going shopping. I want to buy some new jeans.

B Oh yeah. I forgot about that. Is it this weekend?

C I'd love to go. What do you want to see?

D I was just going to call you.

E Don't worry. I'll be there.

F OK. See you then.

G I can't come on Sunday.

H Maybe we could go on Sunday.

Tip strip

Question 16
Read the line below the gap as well as the line above. What does Yolanda need to get?

Question 17
Look for a suggestion. Notice that Maria can't go.

Question 20
This is the end of the conversation. They have agreed what to do.

Questions 21–27

Read the article about a young sailor named Jessica Watson.
Are sentences **21–27** 'Right' (**A**) or 'Wrong' (**B**)?
If there is not enough information to answer 'Right' (**A**) or 'Wrong' (**B**), choose 'Doesn't say' (**C**).
For questions **21–27**, mark **A**, **B** or **C** on your answer sheet.

Jessica Watson – a hero

On 18th October 2009, 16-year-old Jessica Watson set out to do something no one her age had ever done before – to sail around the world alone without any help. She started her trip in Sydney, Australia, on her ten-metre boat and after seven long months alone at sea she finally ended up back in Sydney Harbour on 15th May 2010. As expected, she got a hero's welcome, with thousands of people there to greet her, including 18-year-old Mike Perham. Perham had sailed around the world the previous year at the age of 17.

When she was asked why she wanted to make this difficult journey, Jessica simply answered that she wanted to do something to be proud of. But her trip did not end as well as she had hoped. Instead of listing her as the youngest person to ever sail

around the world alone, the World Speed Sailing Record Council said she needed to have sailed 2000 nautical miles more than she did to break the world record. After hearing this, Jessica wrote in her blog, 'If I haven't been sailing around the world, then it beats me what I've been doing out here all this time.'

Tip strip

Question 21
Jessica started in Sydney and 'ended up back in' where?

Question 22
Look at the starting date in 2009 and the end date in 2010. Is this more or less than 7 months?

Question 23
Does the text say when Jessica's birthday is?

Question 24
Jessica 'got a hero's welcome' and it says how many people went to meet her.

Question 25
Notice how old Mike Perham was when he sailed around the world, not how old he is now.

Question 26
Look at the sentence with '2000 nautical miles' carefully. Did Jessica sail this extra distance or not?

Question 27
Does the text talk about Jessica's future plans?

Example:

0 Jessica is the youngest person to sail around the world.

   A Right   **B** Wrong   **C** Doesn't say

0	A	B	C
	<u> </u>	▭	▭

---

21 Jessica started and ended her trip from the same city.

   A Right   **B** Wrong   **C** Doesn't say

22 Jessica took a little more than seven months to complete the journey.

   A Right   **B** Wrong   **C** Doesn't say

23 Jessica returned to Sydney on the day of her birthday.

   A Right   **B** Wrong   **C** Doesn't say

24 When Jessica arrived back in Sydney, there were many people there to greet her.

   A Right   **B** Wrong   **C** Doesn't say

25 Mike Perham was two years older than Jessica when he sailed around the world.

   A Right   **B** Wrong   **C** Doesn't say

26 Jessica sailed 2000 nautical miles more than anyone else.

   A Right   **B** Wrong   **C** Doesn't say

27 Jessica said she will sail around the world again next year.

   A Right   **B** Wrong   **C** Doesn't say

Questions 28–35

Read the article about the actor, Dakota Fanning.
Choose the best word (**A**, **B** or **C**) for each space.
For questions **28–35**, mark **A**, **B** or **C** on your answer sheet.

Acting since childhood

The actor Dakota Fanning started her acting career at the early age **(0)** .... five. As a child she starred in major films **(28)** .... *War of the Worlds, Charlotte's Web, The Cat in the Hat, Hound Dog,* and as a teenager in the extremely popular Twilight series. She is different from many actors who started acting as children because she **(29)** .... continued her success. **(30)** .... people often wonder what life is like for child actors away from **(31)** .... big screen and the lights. Perhaps it would surprise you to learn that Dakota was a regular teenager. She was a member of the girl scouts and learned **(32)** .... speak French. She loved **(33)** .... films and even collected dolls. She liked to knit and could also play **(34)** .... violin. And her dream was always to be an actor. She doesn't sound much different from most children, does **(35)** .... ?

Example:

| 0 | **A** of | **B** from | **C** at | | 0 | A ▬ | B ▭ | C ▭ |

---

28 **A** as   **B** where   **C** like

29 **A** is   **B** has   **C** will

30 **A** Every   **B** Few   **C** Many

31 **A** a   **B** the   **C** this

32 **A** to   **B** in   **C** from

33 **A** watch   **B** watching   **C** watched

34 **A** a   **B** with   **C** the

35 **A** she   **B** it   **C** they

Tip strip

Question 29
What is the present perfect of *continue*?

Question 30
Which option is for plural countable nouns (such as *people*)?

Question 33
Think of the verb pattern here. Which form follows *love*?

Questions 36–40

Read the descriptions of some words about family and friends.
What is the word for each one?
The first letter is already there. There is one space for each other letter in the word.
For questions **36–40**, write the words on your answer sheet.

Example:

0   This person is your mum or dad's sister.   a _ _ _ _

0	*aunt*

---

36   This is the person who lives next door to you.   n _ _ _ _ _ _ _ _

37   This person is someone you know well and that you like.   f _ _ _ _ _

38   This person is your uncle's child.   c _ _ _ _ _

39   If you have a husband or wife you are this.   m _ _ _ _ _ _

40   This person is invited to visit you in your home.   g _ _ _ _

Questions 36–40
- Read each definition carefully. Is the word a noun, a verb or an adjective?
- Make sure to spell the missing word correctly. You will lose marks for spelling mistakes.

Part 7

Questions 41–50

Complete the email message.
Write ONE word for each space.
For questions **41–50**, write the words on your answer sheet.

Example: | **0** | *was* |

Hi Rob,

I **(0)** .... just thinking about the party on Saturday. Are you **(41)** ....
to bring any music? I need to know so that I can **(42)** .... someone else
to if you can't. I was also thinking about what **(43)** .... said today about
inviting Hannah. I think it's a **(44)** .... idea. I'll invite her tomorrow when
I **(45)** .... her in maths class.
What are you **(46)** .... tomorrow after school? Why don't you come over
to my place to help **(47)** .... with **(48)** .... party arrangements? You
could stay for dinner and my mum could **(49)** .... you home later. Let
me **(50)** ....
Bye for now,
Tom.

Tip strip

Question 41
Think about the future form being used here.

Question 42
Think of a verb to complete this sentence.

Question 43
You need a personal pronoun here.

Question 44
Think of a positive adjective to go with *idea*.

Question 45
You need a verb here.

Question 46
You need the present continuous here.

Question 47
Complete this with a personal pronoun.

Question 48
You need the definite article here.

Question 49
You need a verb that goes with *home* here.

Question 50
Add a word to make a fixed expression.

Part 8

Read the invitation and the text message.
Fill in the information in Katie's notes.
For questions **51–55**, write the information on your answer sheet.

You are invited
to my 12th birthday party
on Sunday 14th May
The party starts at 1 pm

My address is:
63 Porter Street

Let me know if you can come by Friday.
Hope to see you there.

Gina

Katie, are you going to Gina's party on Sunday? Can we go together? Come to my house at 12.30 and my mum can drive us there. She can also pick us up afterwards.
Let me know.
Paul

Katie's notes

Person having party:	*Gina*
Day and date:	**51**
Time:	**52**
Going with:	**53**
Travel there by:	**54**
Be at Paul's at:	**55**

Tip strip

Question 51
Look for a day and a month.

Question 52
Look at the invitation for this information.

Question 53
Who is the text from?

Question 54
The text message says that someone will *drive* them there.

Question 55
This time is in the text message. It is before the party starts.

TEST 1: READING AND WRITING   17

Part 9

Question 56

Read this email message from your friend Matt.

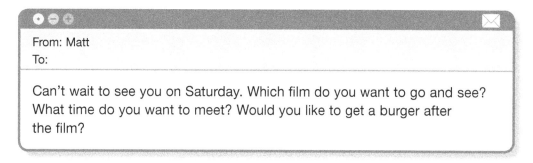

From: Matt
To:

Can't wait to see you on Saturday. Which film do you want to go and see?
What time do you want to meet? Would you like to get a burger after
the film?

Write an email to Matt and answer the questions.
Write **25–35** words.
Write the email on your answer sheet.

Tip strip
Question 56
- Make sure you answer all three questions in the email.
- You need to write between 25 and 35 words, so count them carefully.
- Remember to start with a greeting (e.g. *Hi Matt*) and to add your name to sign off at the end.

Parts 1–5

About the paper

The *Listening* paper lasts for about 30 minutes. It contains five parts with a total of 25 questions, each carrying one mark. It includes texts of varying lengths and could be monologues or dialogues. You will hear each recording twice. You have time to read the questions before you listen. This paper tests your ability to understand texts and identify and write down information.

Part 1

In Part 1, you listen to five short informal conversations. You have to answer one three-option multiple choice question, choosing the correct picture, for each conversation. This part of the paper tests your ability to understand simple facts and important information in a conversation.

Part 2

In Part 2, you listen to a longer informal conversation. You have to match five items with eight options, for example, people with food they like to eat, or days of the week with activities, etc. This part of the paper tests your ability to understand key information in the conversation.

Part 3

In Part 3, you listen to a longer informal or neutral conversation. You have to answer five three-option multiple choice questions. This part of the paper tests your ability to understand key information in the conversation (e.g. numbers, addresses, places, times, dates, names, prices, etc.).

Part 4

In Part 4, you listen to a longer informal or neutral conversation. You are given notes to complete. Five pieces of information are missing. You have to listen and complete the gaps, usually with a single word or number. This part of the paper tests your ability to listen and write down specific information (e.g. numbers, times, dates, prices, spellings and words).

Part 5

In Part 5, you listen to a longer informal or neutral conversation. You are given notes to complete. Five pieces of information are missing. You have to listen and complete the gaps, usually with a single word or number. This part of the paper tests your ability to listen and write down specific information (e.g. numbers, times, dates, prices, spellings and words).

How to do the paper

Part 1

- Before you listen to each extract, look at the pictures and question to prepare you for what you are going to hear.
- The first time you listen, try to get a general understanding and choose the best option. Remember that there may be a reference to all of the options, but only one option answers the question.
- The second time you listen, check carefully to ensure that your answer is correct.

Part 2

- Before you listen, read the instructions, the five items and the eight options to give you a general understanding of what the text will be about.
- Listen carefully for the detail. Remember that there are three options which do not match any of the items.
- Listen again to check that your answer is correct.

Part 3

- Before you listen, read the instructions and the questions.
- Listen carefully for the detail. More than one of the options may be mentioned in the text, but only one of them answers the question.
- Listen again to check that your answer is correct.

Parts 4 and 5

- Before you listen, read the instructions and the notes. Think about the type of information that is missing in each sentence. It may be a word or a number. Occasionally it will be two words.
- Listen and complete the gaps. If you miss a detail, don't worry. Continue onto the next piece of information.
- When you listen a second time, complete any missing information and check your answers.

Questions 1–5

You will hear five short conversations.
You will hear each conversation twice.
There is one question for each conversation.
For each question, choose the right answer (**A**, **B** or **C**).

Example: What time will the boy and girl meet?

A

B

Ⓒ

---

1 How much did the girl pay for her shoes?

A

B

C

2 Which notebook is Jo's?

A

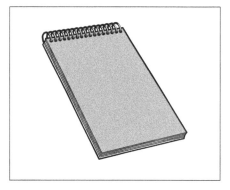

B

C

3 How many children are in Pam's class?

A

B

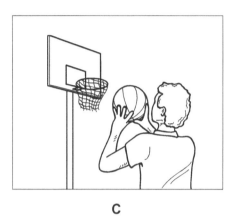

C

4 Which sport will the boy play on Saturday mornings?

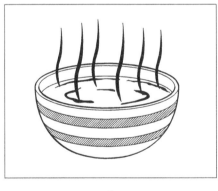

A

B

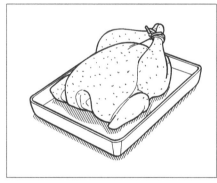

C

5 What will the girl eat for dinner tonight?

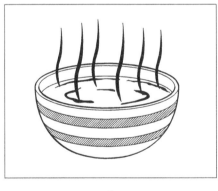

A

B

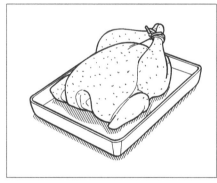

C

Tip strip

Question 1
Listen carefully. The girl gives the correct price at the end of the conversation.

Question 3
The question is about students, not teachers. Pam gives one answer and then she corrects herself.

Question 5
The girl is hoping to eat something else, but in the end, she has what her father says.

Part 2

Questions 6–10

Listen to Pete talking to a friend about his school holiday plans.
What is he doing each day in the second week of his holidays?
For questions **6–10** write a letter **A–H** next to each day.
You will hear the conversation twice.

Example:

0 Monday **B**

DAYS		**PLANNED ACTIVITIES**
6 Tuesday	☐	**A** cinema
7 Wednesday	☐	**B** day trip
8 Thursday	☐	**C** football
9 Friday	☐	**D** homework
10 Saturday	☐	**E** no plans
		F shopping
		G swimming
		H theatre

Tip strip
Questions 6–10
• The boy goes through his plans from Monday – Saturday in order. Listen carefully for the activities listed A–H.
• If you miss an activity, don't worry. You can check it when you listen the second time.

Part 3

Questions 11–15

Listen to Darren talking to a friend about a book report he has to write for school.
For each question, choose the right answer (**A**, **B** or **C**).
You will hear the conversation twice.

Example:

0 Darren and Maria have to write a

   Ⓐ book report.
   B book.
   C story.

---

11 How much of the book has Darren read?

   A all of it
   B none of it
   C half of it

12 The name of the book is

   A *Flight 221.*
   B *Flight 211.*
   C *Flight 212.*

13 Darren returned to school on

   A 20th November.
   B 2nd November.
   C 12th November.

14 When will Darren read the book?

   A tonight
   B at the weekend
   C next week

15 On Sunday, Darren will call Maria at

   A 6.00.
   B 7.15.
   C 7.00.

Tip strip

Question 11
Darren says, 'I haven't actually read the book yet'. Has he read any part of the book?

Question 12
Listen carefully for the number in the title of the book. Check again when you listen for the second time.

Question 13
Darren gives two dates. Listen for the date that is the end of the time he was away from school.

Question 14
Both Darren and Maria say when he will read the book.

Question 15
Darren suggests one time, but Maria tells him a time when she will be home.

Questions 16–20

You will hear a boy asking about an electronic device.
Listen and complete each question.
You will hear the conversation twice.

MP3 Player

The discount is:	*20%*
Price with discount:	**(16)** £
Pay for it on:	**(17)**
Come in before:	**(18)** _____ *o'clock*
Customer's name:	**(19)** *Jack*
Address:	*16 Bond Street*
Phone number:	**(20)**

Tip strip

Questions 16–20
• Read through the text and decide what type of information is missing from each gap.

• Remember that the information will be given in the same order as it appears in the text.

Question 16
Listen for an amount of money in pounds.

Question 17
The assistant agrees that Jack can pay for it on another day. Which day?

Question 18
Jack has to pick it up no later than what time?

Question 19
Jack spells out his surname for the assistant.

Question 20
Jack gives his phone number and the assistant repeats it to check it is correct.

Questions 21–25

You will hear a teacher talking about a school concert.
Listen and complete each question.
You will hear the information twice.

School Concert

Name of school band: *As You Like It*

Day of concert: (21) ....

Be there by: (22) .... *pm*

Band practice: (23) ....
                            and Thursday at 4.00 pm

Room: (24) ....

If you can't come, call: (25) ....

Tip strip

Questions 21–25
- Read through the text and decide what type of information is missing from each gap.
- Remember that the information will be given in the same order as it appears in the text.

Question 21
This information is right at the beginning. Listen for the day.

Question 22
The teacher tells them to be there half an hour before the concert starts. What time is that?

Question 23
The teacher repeats this information to make sure no one forgets.

Question 24
The teacher gives the room number twice and explains where it is.

Question 25
Listen carefully for the phone number which comes at the end. Check again when you listen for the second time.

Parts 1–2

About the paper

The *Speaking* paper lasts for 8–10 minutes. It has two parts and carries a total of 25 marks. There are two candidates and two examiners. One examiner interacts with the candidates and the other examiner acts as the assessor and does not join in the conversation. The candidates are assessed on their performance of the whole test.

Part 1 (5–6 minutes)

In Part 1, the examiner asks you and your partner questions in turn. These are questions about your personal details: your name, where you come from, your family, your studies, etc. This part of the paper tests the language you need to talk to people when you meet them for the first time.

Part 2 (3–4 minutes)

In Part 2, you talk to your partner. The examiner sets up the activity. You and your partner ask and answer questions using information given in the prompt material that the examiner will give you. This part of the paper tests your ability to give factual information of a non-personal kind related to daily life.

How to do the paper

Part 1

- If you don't understand a question, ask the examiner to repeat it. Say *Can you repeat the question, please?* or *Please repeat the question.*
- Try to answer questions about yourself using more than one word.
- If a question begins with *Tell us about* … extend your answer even more. Say as many things as you can about the topic.
- When you are preparing, it will help you to record yourself, so that you can hear what you have done well and what you need to do better.

Part 2

- If you are answering questions, listen to your partner's questions carefully. If you don't understand any questions, it is important that you ask your partner to repeat it or say *I'm sorry I don't understand.*
- Make sure you look at all the information on the card. The questions your partner asks you will not be in the same order as the information that appears on your card.
- If you are asking questions, try to form clear questions that your partner will understand. Use question words like *When? What? Where? How?* etc. to form your questions based on the task card (see example below).
- When you are preparing, it will help you to record yourself, so that you can hear what you have done well and what you need to do better.

Part 1 (5–6 minutes)

Greetings and introductions

At the beginning of Part 1, the examiner greets you and your partner, asks for your names and asks you to spell something.

Giving information about where you are from, what you do, and what you study

The examiner asks you and your partner about where you come from/live, and for information about your school/studies.

Giving general information about yourself

The examiner asks you about your daily life, past experience or future plans. You may be asked about your likes and dislikes, recent experiences or to describe and compare places.

Extended response

In the final section of Part 1, the examiner asks you 'Tell me something about …' for you to give a longer response on a personal topic. You should say at least three things.

Part 2 (3–4 minutes)

[The examiner gives a question card to Candidate B and an answer card to Candidate A]

Candidate A, there is some information about **an athletics club**. *(Turn to page 51)*

Candidate B, you don't know anything about **the athletics club**, so ask **A** some questions about it. *(Turn to page 52)* Now **B**, ask **A** your questions about the athletics club and **A**, you answer them.

[The examiner gives a question card to Candidate A and an answer card to Candidate B]

Candidate B, there is some information about **a music school**. *(Turn to page 52)*

Candidate A, you don't know anything about **the music school**, so ask **B** some questions about it. *(Turn to page 51)* Now **A**, ask **B** your questions about the athletics club and **B**, you answer them.

Tip strip

Part 1

- Practise spelling out your first name and surname so that you can do this easily.
- Practise the pronunciation of school subjects.
- When the examiner says 'Tell me something about …', try to include as much detail as possible.

Part 2

- Listen to your partner and ask him/her to repeat something if you don't understand.
- Look at all the information on the card to prepare for your partner's questions.
- Look at the task card and use question words like *When? What? Where? How?* to form questions.

Practice Test 2

Part 1

Questions 1–5

Which notice (**A–H**) says this (**1–5**)?
For questions **1–5**, mark the correct letter **A–H** on your answer sheet.

Example:

0 You may be late.

0	A	B	C	D	E	F	G	H
	▬	▭	▭	▭	▭	▭	▭	▭

---

1 You must not come in here.

A   DELAYS POSSIBLE

2 You must not walk on here.

B   Talk to people the way you would like people to talk to you

3 You can use these if you pay.

C   Keep out

4 You can do this after a certain time.

D   Keep off the grass

5 You should be nice.

E   Chinese lessons every Monday 3.30–5.30

F   Boats for hire £10 for 30 minutes

G   School library: Use your student card to borrow books

H   No skateboarding during school times

Part 2

Questions 6–10

Read the sentences about a boy called Jamie.
Choose the best word (**A**, **B** or **C**) for each space.
For questions **6–10**, mark **A**, **B** or **C** on your answer sheet.

Example:

0 A new sports club has just opened .... Jamie's school.

   A near   **B** next   **C** close

0	A	B	C
	▬	▢	▢

---

6 At the club, you can play your .... sports, like basketball and table tennis.

   A good   **B** favourite   **C** popular

7 There is a café where you can .... something to eat or drink.

   A take   **B** buy   **C** do

8 Jamie has already become a .... of the club.

   A member   **B** person   **C** athlete

9 He has tried all .... of sports and activities.

   A forms   **B** kinds   **C** things

10 He .... that the sport he likes the most is table tennis.

   A tells   **B** speaks   **C** says

Questions 11–15

Complete the five conversations.
For questions **11–15**, mark **A**, **B** or **C** on your answer sheet.

Example:

0

11 Where is the nearest newsagent's?   **A** I don't think so.

B It's over there.

C I didn't see it.

12 I really love the summer.   **A** I know you have.

B I can't.

C So do I.

13 Do you want to go and see a film?   **A** That's a good idea.

B I don't know it.

C I saw it yesterday.

14 What did you say?   **A** Nothing.

B Sometimes.

C Anything.

15 Can you hear that noise?   **A** I wonder what it is?

B Are you listening?

C I haven't heard anything.

Part 3

Questions 16–20

Complete the phone conversation between a teacher and a student, Wendy.
What does Wendy say to her teacher?
For questions **16–20**, mark the correct letter **A–H** on your answer sheet.

Example:

Teacher: Wendy, have you finished your project?

Wendy: **0** ...A....

0	A	B	C	D	E	F	G	H
	▬	▭	▭	▭	▭	▭	▭	▭

Teacher: Does that mean you don't have it for me?

Wendy: **16** ....

Teacher: Can I ask why?

Wendy: **17** ....

Teacher: Don't tell me you lost the project.

Wendy: **18** ....

Teacher: OK. Don't worry. Can you have it for me on Monday?

Wendy: **19** ....

Teacher: Good. I'll expect it bright and early Monday morning.

Wendy: **20** ....

Teacher: I hope so!

A Actually, I need to speak to you about that.

B That's just it. I haven't finished it yet.

C Thanks, Miss. Don't worry I'll have it for you by then.

D I don't have a computer.

E Don't worry. I can be there on Monday.

F That shouldn't be a problem.

G I did! I started it again but I haven't finished it yet.

H I would have finished it yesterday but my computer crashed.

Questions 21–27

Read the article about three television shows and then answer the questions.
For questions **21–27**, mark **A**, **B** or **C** on your answer sheet.

The Artist in You

The Artist in You is a new show for kids and teenagers. Each week, Tony Moldino, an artist himself, shows you how to make an amazing work of art. Last week, it was painting a portrait. This week it's drawing with pencil on paper, and next week it's how to use your digital camera to take great pictures. It's on every Tuesday at 5.00 pm.

Dance School

Dance School is a new teen drama about a group of students who all want to become dancers. It follows their lives in a school for dancers in New York. The story is told through the eyes of Tina Giles, a farm girl who dreams of becoming a ballerina. On her first day at the school she meets Joe, Heather and John. Together they try hard to achieve their dream. *Dance School* is on every Monday night at 7.00.

Bert

Bert is a new comedy cartoon series for older kids. It follows the funny times of Bert and his family in a small town in America. Each episode is a new story. In this week's episode, Bert's younger sister gets a part in the school play. Bert isn't happy because he too wants to be in the play. He does everything he can think of to get his wish! Bert is on every Wednesday at 6.00 pm.

Example:

0 *The Artist in You*

    A began this year.
    B is an old show.
    C is a show for artists.

---

21 Every week on the show *The Artist in You*, you can

    A learn to draw.
    B learn to paint.
    C learn something new.

22 Tony Moldino is on the show

    A this week only.
    B every week.
    C next week only.

23 *Dance School* is a show about

    A a girl called Tina Giles.
    B a new school.
    C a group of young dancers.

24 Tina Giles grew up

    A in a city.
    B in a village.
    C on a farm.

25 Tina met her school friends for the first time

    A on a farm.
    B at her new school.
    C years ago.

26 *Bert* is a show about

    A students.
    B a family.
    C an American town.

27 Bert is unhappy because

    A his sister is in the school play.
    B he isn't in the school play.
    C he doesn't like school.

Questions 28–35

Read the article about the Tasmanian Devil.
Choose the best word (**A**, **B** or **C**) for each space.
For questions **28–35**, mark **A**, **B** or **C** on your answer sheet.

The Tasmanian devil

The Tasmanian devil is an unusual animal found only **(0)** .... the island of Tasmania in the southeast of Australia. **(28)** .... people know the devil from the popular cartoon character, Taz, but this little animal is in fact a real animal. What does a real devil look **(29)** .... ? It is the size of a small black dog and just as cute. **(30)** .... don't let its size fool you. The devil can bite! In the wild, it is a carnivore, which means it **(31)** .... eat other animals. It **(32)** .... not often kill the animals it eats though. Rather, it eats animals that have **(33)** .... died from some other cause.

Like many other Australian animals, these little black animals are marsupials. This means **(34)** .... like kangaroos, for example, they carry their babies in a pouch. Surprisingly, the mother devil **(35)** .... look after four little babies at a time!

Example:

0 A on	B in	C at		0	A ▬	B ▭	C ▭

---

28 A Every   **B** Each   **C** Most

29 A as   **B** like   **C** of

30 A But   **B** And   **C** So

31 A has   **B** must   **C** will

32 A does   **B** do   **C** doing

33 A since   **B** yet   **C** already

34 A which   **B** that   **C** when

35 A does   **B** has   **C** can

Part 6

Questions 36–40

Read the descriptions of some things that you can find at school and at home.
What is the word for each one?
The first letter is already there. There is one space for each other letter in the word.
For questions **36–40**, write the words on your answer sheet.

Example:

0   This is the place where you have your lessons.   c _ _ _ _ _ _ _ _ | **0** | *classroom* |

36   This is what you study at school.   s _ _ _ _ _ _

37   In some schools, students have to wear this.   u _ _ _ _ _ _

38   This person helps you learn things.   t _ _ _ _ _ _

39   You do this study away from school.   h _ _ _ _ _ _ _

40   If you don't know a word, you can look it up in this.   d _ _ _ _ _ _ _ _ _

Part 7

Questions 41–50

Complete these emails.
Write ONE word for each space.
For questions **41–50**, write the words on your answer sheet.

Example: **0** | *where*

Dear Miss Peachey,

Can you please let me know **(0)** .... I can buy the class reader
from? I tried **(41)** .... buy it from the bookshop near my house but
they **(42)** .... have it. I would **(43)** .... to buy it by Friday so that
(44) .... can have it in **(45)** .... lesson.
Yours,
Tania.

Dear Tania,
You'll find it **(46)** .... Cheap Books. **(47)** .... is a store in the
shopping centre across **(48)** .... road from school. Try to get
(49) .... by Friday **(50)** .... you will need to read some of it
over the weekend.
Best wishes,
B. Peachey

Questions 51–55

Read the school notice and the email.
Fill in the information in the application form.
For questions **51–55**, write the information on your answer sheet.

SCHOOL PLAY
Romeo and Juliet

*Are you interested in trying out
for the school play?*

Come to room 24B
on Friday at 3.30 pm.

Complete the form below
and bring it with you on Friday.

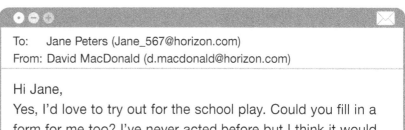

To: Jane Peters (Jane_567@horizon.com)
From: David MacDonald (d.macdonald@horizon.com)

Hi Jane,
Yes, I'd love to try out for the school play. Could you fill in a form for me too? I've never acted before but I think it would be a lot of fun to try. I'd like to try out for Romeo. Wouldn't it be great if I got the part of Romeo and you got Juliet? Anyway, my home number is 987 6541. See you on Friday!
David

SCHOOL PLAY application form

Name of play:	*Romeo and Juliet*
Time of audition:	**51**
Full name:	**52**
Acting experience:	**53**
Phone number:	**54**
Email address:	**55**

Part 9

Question 56

You are going out. Leave a note for your parents. Tell them:

- **where** you are going.
- **who** you are going with.
- **what time** you will be home.

Write **25–35** words.
Write the note on your answer sheet.

Part 1

Questions 1–5

You will hear five short conversations.
You will hear each conversation twice.
There is one question for each conversation.
For each question, choose the right answer (**A**, **B** or **C**).

Example: Where did the boy go on holiday?

| A | B | C |

---

1 What's the weather going to be like tomorrow?

| A | B | C |

2 Where are the boys going to meet their friend?

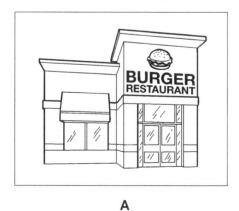 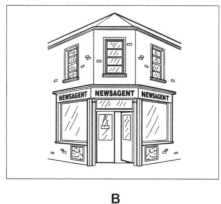 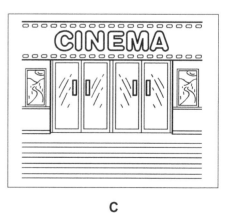

| A | B | C |

3   Which card does Nicole buy?

A

B

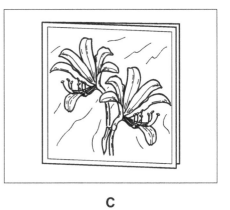

C

4   How many chocolate ice creams does the boy want?

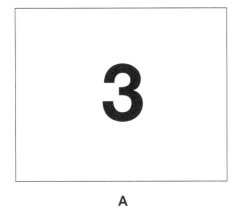

A

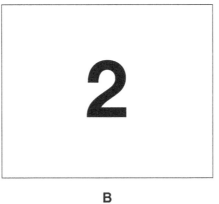

B

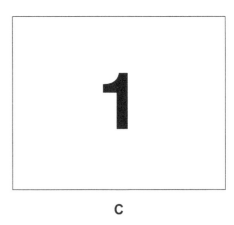

C

5   What time did Patrick say he would be home?

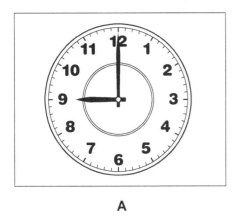

A

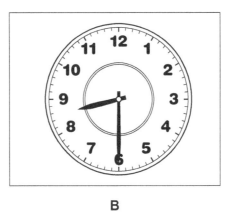

B

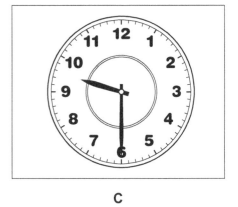

C

Part 2

Questions 6–10

Listen to Rita talking to a friend about her family's hobbies.
What hobby does each person have?
For questions **6–10** write a letter **A–H** next to each person.
You will hear the conversation twice.

Example:

0   Cousin   [A]

PEOPLE

6   Sister   ☐

7   Brother   ☐

8   Mum   ☐

9   Dad   ☐

10   Granddad   ☐

HOBBIES

A   collecting stamps

B   cycling

C   fishing

D   football

E   golf

F   skiing

G   swimming

H   tennis

Part 3

Questions 11–15

Listen to Ruben talking to a friend about something new he wants to buy.
For each question, choose the right answer (**A**, **B**, or **C**).
You will hear the conversation twice.

Example:

0 Ruben is going to buy a

    Ⓐ laptop.
    B desktop computer.
    C mobile phone.

---

11 He is going to buy it from

    A Computer Warehouse.
    B the supermarket.
    C Frank's Computers.

12 The shop is on

    A Elizabeth Street.
    B Mersey Road.
    C Mary Street.

13 How much is it going to cost?

    A £500
    B £550
    C £600

14 His mum will pick it up

    A on Saturday.
    B tonight.
    C on Friday night.

15 On Saturday, Ruben's friend will visit him at

    A 10 o'clock.
    B 11 o'clock.
    C 1 o'clock.

Questions 16–20

You will hear a girl asking about music lessons.
Listen and complete each question.
You will hear the conversation twice.

Music lessons

Instrument: *piano*

Day: **(16)** ....

Time: **(17)** ....

Price per lesson: **(18)** £ ....

Address of music school: **(19)** ....

Teacher's mobile number: **(20)** ....

Questions 21–25

You will hear some information about a play.
Listen and complete each question.
You will hear the information twice.

Play

Name: *The Princess and the Frog*

Days: **(21)** .... *and Sunday*

Play starts at: **(22)** ....

Be at theatre at: **(23)** ....

Price for children: **(24)** ....

To book tickets, call: **(25)** ....

Part 1 (5–6 minutes)

Greetings and introductions

At the beginning of Part 1, the examiner greets you and your partner, asks for your names and asks you to spell something.

Giving information about where you are from, what you do, and what you study

The examiner asks you and your partner about where you come from/live, and for information about your school/studies.

Giving general information about yourself

The examiner asks you about your daily life, past experience or future plans. You may be asked about your likes and dislikes, recent experiences or to describe and compare places.

Extended response

In the final section of Part 1, the examiner asks you 'Tell me something about …' for you to give a longer response on a personal topic. You should say at least three things.

Part 2 (3–4 minutes)

[The examiner gives a question card to Candidate B and an answer card to Candidate A]

Candidate A: there is some information about **a birthday party.** *[Turn to page 51.]*

Candidate B: you don't know anything about **the birthday party**, so ask **A** some questions about it. *[Turn to page 52.]* Now **B**, ask **A** your questions about the birthday party and **A**, you answer them.

[The examiner gives a question card to Candidate A and an answer card to Candidate B]

Candidate B: there is some information about **a bookshop**. *[Turn to page 52.]*

Candidate A: you don't know anything about the bookshop, so ask **B** some questions about it. *[Turn to page 51.]* Now **A**, ask **B** your questions about the birthday party and **B**, you answer them.

Speaking Bank

Part 1: General conversation

In this part of the test, the examiner will ask you a few questions about you and your life. Be prepared to give suitable answers on topics such as your name, where you live, your family, your studies, your daily life, likes and dislikes, etc.

Talking about yourself

I'm good at …

I really like/don't like …

I enjoy/love …

I'm not good at …

I don't like/enjoy …

My favourite … is …

There are three people in my family.

Explaining

I mean …

Giving reasons

because …

Giving your opinion

I think/don't think …

I believe/don't believe …

Asking the examiner for clarification

Can you repeat that, please?

Sorry, what did you say?

Did you say … ?

What is … ?

Exam help

- Extend your answers. Say more than just one word.

- Ask the examiner to repeat if you have not understood.

- If you can't remember the word for something, say it another way.

Part 2: Asking and answering questions

In this part of the test, you will have to ask and answer questions with your partner about a situation based on pictures and written prompts.

Asking for information

Price

How much is the student ticket?

How much does it cost?

Address

Where is it?

What is the address?

Name

What is the name of the school/shop/etc.?

Email/phone

What is the email address?

What is the phone number?

Dates/days/times

When is/are the … ?

Is it open/closed on Mondays, etc.?

What time does it open/close?

What time is it on?

Other information

What can you do/learn there?

What can you win?

Is it for children/teenagers?

Does it sell … ?

Can you buy … ?

What can you see there?

Is there a car park?

Answering questions

Yes/No questions

Positive answers   Yes, it is.

Yes, you can.

Yes, it's …

Yes, it's open on Mondays, etc.

Yes, the phone number is …

Yes, the email address is …

Negative answers   No, it isn't.

No, you can't.

Wh- questions

The name of … is …

The address is …

It's in … Street.

It's on … Road.

The phone number is …

The email address is …

Asking your partner for clarification

Can you repeat (your question), please?

Sorry, what did you say?

I don't understand what you mean.

Do you mean … ?

- When you ask questions, think of the type of information you need and then choose the right question word.

- When you answer questions, ask your partner for clarification if you have not understood.

Writing Bank

Part 9: Email or postcard

Example question

Read the email from your English friend, Matt.

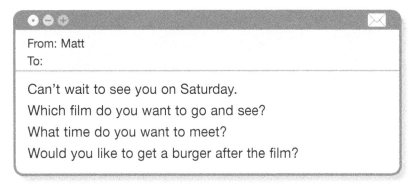

From: Matt
To:

Can't wait to see you on Saturday.

Which film do you want to go and see?

What time do you want to meet?

Would you like to get a burger after the film?

Write an email to Matt and answer the questions.
Write **25–35** words.
Write the email on your answer sheet.

Example answer

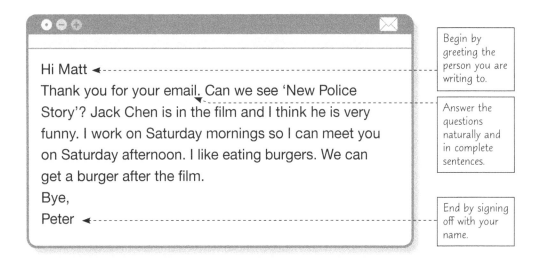

Hi Matt ◄------------------------------ Begin by greeting the person you are writing to.

Thank you for your email. Can we see 'New Police Story'? Jack Chen is in the film and I think he is very funny. I work on Saturday mornings so I can meet you on Saturday afternoon. I like eating burgers. We can get a burger after the film.

Answer the questions naturally and in complete sentences.

Bye,

Peter ◄------------------------------ End by signing off with your name.

Exam help

- Imagine you are writing to someone you know well. Think of interesting ways to answer his/her questions.

- Use short forms, e.g. 'I've just painted' not 'I have just painted'.

- Greet them and say goodbye in a friendly way.

- Make sure you communicate your message as clearly as possible.

- Check you have written between 25 and 35 words.

Part 9: Notice

You have lost your new mobile phone. Write a notice to put on the wall at your school.

Say:

* **where** you lost your mobile phone.
* **what** your mobile phone looks like.
* **how** to return it to you.

Write **25-35** words.
Write the notice on your answer sheet.

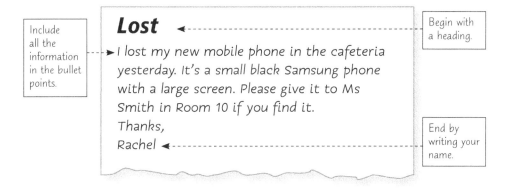

Include all the information in the bullet points.

Lost

I lost my new mobile phone in the cafeteria yesterday. It's a small black Samsung phone with a large screen. Please give it to Ms Smith in Room 10 if you find it.
Thanks,
Rachel

Begin with a heading.

End by writing your name.

* Give your notice a heading and underline it, e.g. Lost.
* Include all the information in the bullet points.
* Be clear about what you want to communicate.

* End the notice with your name.
* Make sure you communicate your message as clearly as possible.
* Check you have written between 25 and 35 words.

Part 9: Note

Example question

You are going out. Leave a note for your parents. Tell them:

- **where** you are going.
- **who** you are going with.
- **what** time you will be home.

Write **25-35** words.
Write the note on your answer sheet.

Example answer

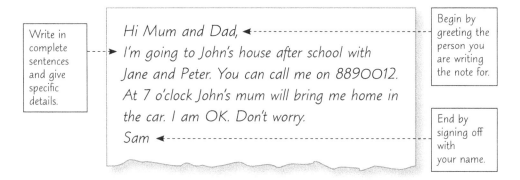

Write in complete sentences and give specific details.

Begin by greeting the person you are writing the note for.

Hi Mum and Dad,
I'm going to John's house after school with Jane and Peter. You can call me on 8890012. At 7 o'clock John's mum will bring me home in the car. I am OK. Don't worry.
Sam

End by signing off with your name.

Exam help

- Imagine you are writing to someone you know well or to a member of your family.
- Give some specific details about the things, people or places you talk about.
- Greet and say goodbye to the person you are writing a note for in a friendly way.

- Write in complete sentences and give specific details.
- Use short forms, e.g. 'I'm going to the cinema' not 'I am going to the cinema'.
- Make sure you communicate your message as clearly as possible.
- Check you have written between 25 and 35 words.

Visuals for Speaking Tests

Student A

Test 1, Part 2 (page 27)

Junior Athletics Club
56 James Street

Are you 10–16 years old?
Come and join our athletics club.

Training: Mondays and Wednesdays 4–6 pm
Visit: www.athletics.com

Alan's music school

- where/school?
- what/learn?
- cost?
- when/classes?
- phone number?

Test 2, Part 2 (page 45)

Max's Birthday Party
You are invited to
Max's birthday party

Sunday 5th June at 1 pm
63 Green Street
Let me know if you can come.
Call me on 456 7890.

Bookshop

- name/bookshop?
- open/Sunday?
- time/open?
- sell/schoolbooks?
- phone number?

Test 1, Part 2 (page 27)

Athletics club

- name/club?
- for children?
- website?
- when/training?
- address?

Alan's music school
Smith Street Shopping Centre

*We'll teach you to play
guitar, piano or the drums.
Classes 3 to 5 pm every Saturday*

Fee: £5 per lesson
Phone: 265 0828

Test 2, Part 2 (page 45)

Birthday Party

- name/boy?
- when/party?
- time/party?
- phone number?
- address?

Pete's Books
117 Jones Street

Get your schoolbooks here.

Open seven days a week
9 am – 5 pm.
Telephone: 267 8911

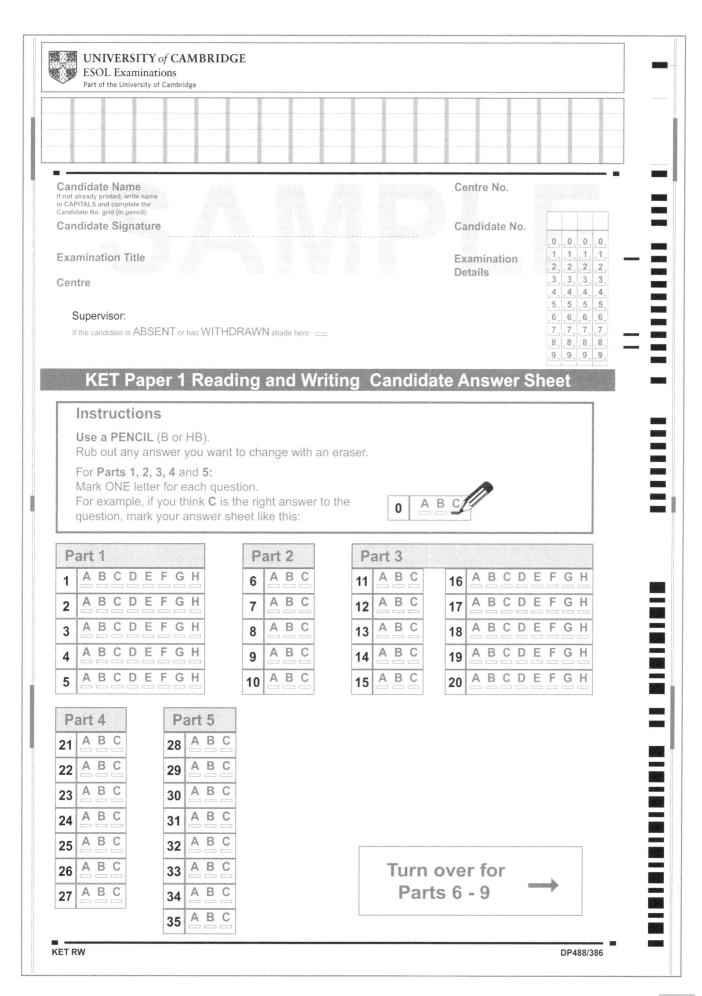

UNIVERSITY of CAMBRIDGE
ESOL Examinations
Part of the University of Cambridge

Candidate Name
If not already printed, write name in CAPITALS and complete the Candidate No. grid (in pencil).

Candidate Signature

Examination Title

Centre

Supervisor:
If the candidate is ABSENT or has WITHDRAWN shade here ⬚

Centre No.

Candidate No.

Examination Details

KET Paper 1 Reading and Writing Candidate Answer Sheet

Instructions

Use a PENCIL (B or HB).
Rub out any answer you want to change with an eraser.

For **Parts 1, 2, 3, 4** and **5:**
Mark ONE letter for each question.
For example, if you think **C** is the right answer to the question, mark your answer sheet like this:

0   A B C

Part 1
1 A B C D E F G H
2 A B C D E F G H
3 A B C D E F G H
4 A B C D E F G H
5 A B C D E F G H

Part 2
6 A B C
7 A B C
8 A B C
9 A B C
10 A B C

Part 3
11 A B C
12 A B C
13 A B C
14 A B C
15 A B C
16 A B C D E F G H
17 A B C D E F G H
18 A B C D E F G H
19 A B C D E F G H
20 A B C D E F G H

Part 4
21 A B C
22 A B C
23 A B C
24 A B C
25 A B C
26 A B C
27 A B C

Part 5
28 A B C
29 A B C
30 A B C
31 A B C
32 A B C
33 A B C
34 A B C
35 A B C

Turn over for
Parts 6 - 9 →

KET RW

DP488/386

For **Parts 6, 7 and 8:**

Write your answers in the spaces next to the numbers (36 to 55) like this:

0	example

Part 6	Do not write here
36	1 36 0
37	1 37 0
38	1 38 0
39	1 39 0
40	1 40 0

Part 7	Do not write here
41	1 41 0
42	1 42 0
43	1 43 0
44	1 44 0
45	1 45 0
46	1 46 0
47	1 47 0
48	1 48 0
49	1 49 0
50	1 50 0

Part 8	Do not write here
51	1 51 0
52	1 52 0
53	1 53 0
54	1 54 0
55	1 55 0

Part 9 (Question 56): Write your answer below.

Do not write below (Examiner use only).
0 1 2 3 4 5

ANSWER SHEETS

Reproduced with kind permission from Cambridge English Language Assessment

CAMBRIDGE ENGLISH
Language Assessment
Part of the University of Cambridge

Candidate Name
If not already printed, **write name**
in CAPITALS and complete the
Candidate No. grid (**in pencil**).

Candidate Signature

Examination Title

Centre

Supervisor:

If the candidate is ABSENT or has WITHDRAWN shade here

Centre No.

Candidate No.

Examination
Details

0	0	0	0
1	1	1	1
2	2	2	2
3	3	3	3
4	4	4	4
5	5	5	5
6	6	6	6
7	7	7	7
8	8	8	8
9	9	9	9

KET Paper 2 Listening Candidate Answer Sheet

Instructions

Use a PENCIL (B or HB).

Rub out any answer you want to change with an eraser.

For **Parts 1, 2** and **3:**
Mark ONE letter for each question.
For example, if you think **C** is the right answer to the
question, mark your answer sheet like this:

0   A B C

Part 1		Part 2		Part 3	
1	A B C	**6**	A B C D E F G H	**11**	A B C
2	A B C	**7**	A B C D E F G H	**12**	A B C
3	A B C	**8**	A B C D E F G H	**13**	A B C
4	A B C	**9**	A B C D E F G H	**14**	A B C
5	A B C	**10**	A B C D E F G H	**15**	A B C

For **Parts 4** and **5:**
Write your answers in the spaces next to the
numbers (16 to 25) like this:

0   example

Part 4		Do not write here	Part 5		Do not write here
16		1 16 0	**21**		1 21 0
17		1 17 0	**22**		1 22 0
18		1 18 0	**23**		1 23 0
19		1 19 0	**24**		1 24 0
20		1 20 0	**25**		1 25 0

KET L

DP741/088

KET for Schools Top 20 Questions

1. **What is the format of the KET for Schools exam, and are all the papers taken on the same day?**
   There are three papers:
   1 Reading and Writing (1 hour 10 minutes)
   2 Listening (about 30 minutes)
   3 Speaking (8–10 minutes)
   Papers 1 and 2 are always taken on the same day. The Speaking test may be taken on the same day or on a different day.

2. **How is KET for Schools different from KET?**
   KET for Schools follows the same format as KET. The difference is that the content and topics in KET for Schools are more suitable for the interests and experiences of younger people.

3. **What level is KET for Schools?**
   KET is aligned to the Council of Europe Common European Framework of Reference (CEFR). KET is level A2 in the CEFR.

4. **Is KET for Schools suitable for teenagers from any culture?**
   Yes. All tasks are written to avoid any cultural bias.

5. **How many marks are needed to pass the exam?**
   Pass with merit = 85–100%
   Pass = 70–84%
   A1 = 45–69%

6. **Do I have to pass each paper in order to pass the exam?**
   No. Each paper doesn't have a pass or fail mark. The final mark a candidate gets in KET for Schools is an average mark obtained by adding the marks for all three papers together.

7. **What mark do I need to get to pass the exam overall?**
   To achieve a pass in the KET for Schools exam a candidate must receive a minimum of 70% as an overall average.

8. **Can I use pens or pencils in the exam?**
   In KET for Schools a candidate must use a pencil in all papers.

9. **If I write entirely in capital letters, does this affect my score?**
   No. Candidates are not penalised for writing in capitals in the exam.

10. **Am I allowed to use a dictionary?**
    No.

11. **Is correct spelling important in Paper 1 (Reading and Writing)?**
    It is important only in Parts 6, 7 and 8.

12. **Is correct spelling important in Paper 2 (Listening)?**
    It is important only in Parts 4 and 5.

13. **In Paper 1 (Reading and Writing) will extra time be given for me to transfer my answers to the answer sheet?**
    No. You must do this in the 1 hour and 10 minutes you are given to complete the exam.

14. **In Paper 2 (Listening) will extra time be given for me to transfer my answers to the answer sheet?**
    Yes. You will be given some time at the end of the test for this.

15. **How many times will I hear each recording in Paper 2 (Listening)?**
    You will hear each recording twice.

16. **Can I ask any questions if I don't understand something in Papers 1 (Reading and Writing) and 2 (Listening)?**
    The only questions you can ask are those that relate to the rules of the exam. For example, the time you have, where to write your name or your answers, completing the answer sheet, whether or not you can use a pen, etc. You cannot ask for any help with the test items themselves.

17. **Can I ask any questions if I don't understand something in Paper 3 (Speaking)?**
    Yes. You can ask the examiner to repeat a question in Part 1 and to repeat the instructions in Part 2. If you still don't understand, tell the examiner you don't understand. You can ask your partner to repeat or clarify when they are asking you questions or answering your questions in Part 2.

18. **In Paper 3 (Speaking), do I have to go in with another student? Can I choose my partner?**
    You cannot be examined alone. You will usually be examined with one other candidate, but if you are one of the last candidates to be examined and there is an odd number of candidates on the day, you may be examined in a group of three. In some smaller centres you may be able to choose your partner, but in bigger centres this may not be possible.

19. **In Paper 3 (Speaking), is it a good idea to prepare what I am going to say in Part 1?**
    It's a good idea to practise saying your name, spelling your surname and talking about yourself (your family, school, school subjects, hobbies, etc.). It is important that you answer the examiner's questions and that you do so naturally, so listen carefully and think about the questions you have been asked. If you give a prepared speech you may not answer the examiner's question. You will lose marks if your answers are irrelevant.

20. **In Paper 3 (Speaking), what if I can't understand my partner in Part 2 or if he/she can't understand me?**
    If there is a communication breakdown between you and your partner in Part 2, try to solve the problem between you. For example, ask your partner for clarification or to repeat a question or an answer, or help your partner if necessary. You will be given credit for helping your partner if he/she is having difficulty.